Can I Come Down Now
Dad?

— JOHN HEGLEY —————

Can I Come Down Now Dad?

with drawings by the author

Mandarin

also by John Hegley

Glad to Wear Glasses

CAN I COME DOWN NOW DAD?

First published in Great Britain in 1991
by Methuen London
This edition published 1992
by Mandarin Paperbacks
Michelin House, 81 Fulham Road, London SW3 6RB

Copyright © 1989, 1990, 1991 by John Hegley
The author has asserted his moral rights

A CIP catalogue record for this book
is available from the British Library

ISBN 0 7493 1147 9

Some of these poems have previously
appeared in the *Weekend Guardian*.

Printed and bound in Great Britain
by Cox and Wyman Ltd, Cardiff Road, Reading

Contents

Luton	1
When the Queen came to Luton	2
Super sunburn	3
My Dad's new belt	4
Eddie don't like furniture	5
My doggie don't wear glasses	7
Memory	7
Reflection	7
Pet	8
Pat	9
On the ward	10
Colin	11
John Hegarty's cap	12
These National Health glasses	13
In the arms of my glasses	13
The briefcase	14
Go and play in the middle	16
A comparison of logs and dogs	17
In the name of the Lord	18
The hearing difficulty	19
On the booze	20
He saw his dinner on TV	21
Steamed pudding	23
Bad news	25
One day while we were getting out our rough books	26
The martian	27
The play	27
The snub	27
The scouting outing	28
Dad's dark glasses	30
The wizard that was	31

The genie in the wireless 32
Mr McNaulty 34
Train spotters 35
Well bred dog 37
Well executed poem 38
Electric chair poem 38
I am going 39
On the bus 40
Poetry 41
String 42
My old cap 43
Going to Virgin Records 44
A spectacular tale 45
A walk around the house 47
Smothering Sunday 48
The Easter Story according to St Bernard 49
On Hampstead Heath 50
What we have been 50
The photos of the divorce 51
Making confetti 51
Train window pain 52
Off the rails 53
Camping for pleasure 54
In Edinburgh 55
Christmas in the doghouse 56
God plays I Spy 58
The miracle and the people 58
The Romans 59
Watling Street 60
Digging for it 61
The pillars of the gods 62

Sat on the Pillar of Hercules   62
Forever Roman   63
Gaul   64
A centurion has a bit of fun   65
The Roman ruins of Chester   66
The Coliseum   68
The Roman showm'n   69
Togas   70
St George's Day poem   71
A dog's complaint   73
Haircut in Seville   74
Sketches of Portugal   75
A Barrow escape   76
On the Isle of Man   76
Grange-over-Sands   77
Bury St Edmunds   78
A childhood hobby   79
First sex   79
Lucky Bags   80
Scottish country dancing   83
At home   84
Plasticine glasses   85
Sheds   86
Can I come down now Dad?   87
The stand up comedian sits down   88

___ Luton ___

(a poem about the town of my upbringing and the conflict between my working-class origins and the middle-class status conferred upon me by a university education)

I remember Luton
as I'm swallowing my crout'n

When the Queen came to Luton

I felt awkward
seeing my mother openly overjoyed and childlike
shaking her flag
and making a din
and advising me to do the same
if I didn't want a good hiding
when my father came in

___ Super sunburn _____

super sunburn
is what my brother
called the bright right handprints
that my Dad would add to my arms and legs
when I was bad
he thought up the title
one night while he was eating my supper
regular burns were handed out
for shouting at my sister
when she failed to collect the rent
after I had landed on one of her properties in Monopoly
but the biggest attack
was for when my Dad said he was fed up
to the back teeth with me
and I pointed out that he never had any back teeth
my brother said that the marks I received on this occasion
were excellent

My Dad's new belt

when my Dad bought his new belt
the woman who sold it to him
told him that it was very strong
and would probably last longer than he would
and my Dad said that he would give it to one of his
  children

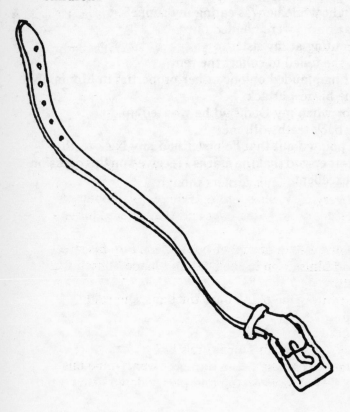

Eddie don't like furniture

Eddie don't go for sofas or settees
or those little tables that you have to buy in threes
the closest thing that Eddie's got to an article of
    furniture's
the cheese board
Eddie doesn't bolster the upholstery biz
there's a lot of furniture in the world but none of it's
    Eddie's
he won't have it in the house however well it's made
Eddie's bedroom was fully furnished
when the floorboards had been laid
and Eddie played guitar
until he decided that his guitar was far too like
an article of furniture
Eddie offers visitors a corner of the room
you get used to the distances between you pretty soon
but with everyone in corners though
it isn't very easy when you're trying to play pontoon
he once got in a rowing boat and they offered him a
    seat
it was just a strip of timber but it wasn't up his street
he stood himself up in the boat and made himself feel
    steady
then he threw the plank onto the bank and said
furniture?
no thank you
when it's on a bonfire furniture's fine
any time that Eddie gets a number twenty-nine bus
even if there's seats on top and plenty down below

Eddie always goes where the pushchairs go
does Eddie like furniture?
I don't think so
if you go round Eddie's place and have a game of
    hide and seek
it isn't very long before you're found
and in a fit of craziness Eddie took the legs off his dash
    hound
that stopped him dashing around
Eddie quite likes cutlery
but he don't like furniture
if you give him some for Christmas
he'll returniture

___ My doggie don't wear glasses ___

my doggie don't wear glasses
so they're lying when they say
a dog looks like its owner
aren't they

___ Memory ___

my sister loved animals
she was always taking the dog out
and stroking it
and the goldfish

___ Reflection ___

my Mum used to spend so long cleaning the
  mirror
you could see her face in it
(if you used your imagination)

Pet

John was feeling a bit lonely
so he decided to pretend that his portable telly was a
　　little dog
the screen was its face
the cable was its tail
the aerial was its ear
and the screws at the back
they were its little fleas
John was very happy with his new friend
until one day she became very ill
after John had given her a bath
when the repair man came
John called out IT'S ALL RIGHT PET
THE VET'S HERE!
and the repair man asked John if he was sick
and John explained that it was not him that was sick
it was his little dog
and when he led the man into the living room
and showed him the portable telly all wrapped up in
　　blankets
the repair man took out a big screwdriver
and pushed it into John's throat
oh great said John
you're going to get rid of her little fleas as well are you?
but the repair man thought he was teasing
and he took hold of John and he hit him
and the portable telly jumped up and bit him

___ Pat _____

I said Pat
you are fat
and you are cataclysmically desirable
and to think I used to think
that slim was where it's at
well not any more Pat
you've changed that
you love yourself
you flatter yourself
you shatter their narrow image of the erotic
and Pat said
what do you mean FAT?

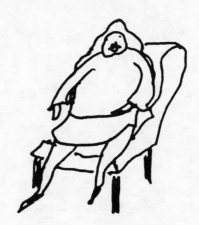

On the ward

once when I worked in a hospital
one boy chewed the wheels
of another boy's wheelchair so badly
that it rolled along very lumpily
and had to be sent to the menders

___ Colin ___

Colin was a vandal and when certain things were said
he flew off the handle and he banged you in the head
he went down the hospital to get it sorted out
the doctor said good morning and Colin knocked
    him out
Colin said I'm sorry doctor can you make me sane
the doctor said we'll sort you out and took out Colin's brain
cell
when Colin left the hospital he was miserable
what was he to do instead of banging people in the head?
but then one day he walked into a lamp-post in the street
and discovered self expression aggravating concrete
soon he was as right as rain
and he couldn't complain at all
he got himself a little job as a demolition ball
now Colin does a hard day's work
comes home at half past five
calls out Mum it's me I'm home and I'm still alive
then he runs into the living room
gets stuck into the wall
and his Mum says show some consideration Colin
do it in the hall
and by the way your dinner's in the safe

John Hegarty's cap

one day I came home from school
and my Mum said that cap's not yours
and sure enough it was not
it was John Hegarty's
a boy with a name like mine
and a cap like mine
you don't know where it's been she said
throwing it onto the fire

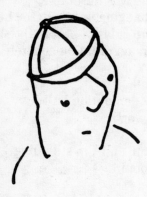

These National Health glasses

these national health glasses were devised
before the vision of the people got privatised

In the arms of my glasses

they can call me softy
as ofty
as they please
but still I'll stand by these
my little optical accessories
they stop me walking into lamp-posts
and trees
when it's foggy
and I'm out walking with my doggie

The briefcase

from the very beginning I loved my glasses
the eye test made me feel important
I wanted to be colour blind as well
for some reason
I was never teased about them as a child
not even at the grammar school
where daily they would mock my briefcase
because it was not made of leather
as I recall there was only ever one boyhood jibe
aimed at my glasses
and this a fairly oblique one
oi double glazing
where did you get that plastic briefcase?
in adult years I got a lot more trouble
on one occasion
a rabble
threw rubble
at my glasses
it was after this that I decided to take action
I bought myself a leather briefcase
and the next day set out to face my building site
    tormentors
somehow the briefcase in my hand
was a stand
against a land

which had gradually lost its magic for me
a joyful absurdity
in the face
of the tragically commonplace
as I approached the contractors
for once it felt like MY world again
what have you got in the briefcase then four eyes?
was the question
POWER was the reply
the power of the human imagination
and I walked proudly
and steadily past them
in a shower of flying masonry

Go and play in the middle

my Mum used to watch out of the window
these boys who played football
on the green in front of our bungalow
she used to stand well back
so she couldn't be seen
and when the ball hit the wall of our garden
she said to my Dad
it's hit our wall again Bob
go out and tell them
and my Dad would go out and tell them
maybe eight or nine times in a day
to go and play in the middle
and immediately he had told them
my Mum would be on the watch
for the next time he would need sending out
and sometimes it was only a few moments
after he had come back in

A comparison of logs and dogs

both are very popular at Christmas
but it is not generally considered cruel
to abandon a log
and dogs are rarely used as fuel

Loggie

___ In the name of the Lord _____

J   just like his Dad

E   ever so just (like his Dad)

S   specless (he never wore glasses)

U   unable to swim

S   sometimes I wonder if he was praying for
the betraying kiss of Judas so as not to miss out
on his Easter egg

C   cut bread into very thin slices

H   hippy aeroplane impressionist

R   really easy to spot in a crowd on a Good Friday

I   I wonder if he had a dog

S   escapologist

T   took him three days but he did it

The hearing difficulty

when she was about nine
unbeknown to the rest of the family
my sister filled in a newspaper coupon
requesting further information
from a hearing aid company in London
and a representative travelled the thirty-two miles
to our home in Luton
to give more information about the product
realising that it was not enough to say 'not today
    thank you'
or 'we're not interested in God'
my mother burst into the living room
where Angela and I were playing Monopoly
and demanded an explanation for the preposterous
    arrival
Angela said there was a girl in her class
who was a bit deaf
and she thought a little hearing aid would be of help
my mother then dragged her out to the front door
to repeat the story
so the man could see that he was dealing with an idiot

On the booze

My dad very rarely drank
but one time when he did
my mother blew her lid rather
and leaving the lather
and the sink
she said you stink
you stink of drink
you've tried to hide it with a peppermint
but I don't think it's done the job
because you blinking stink Bob
it's obnoxious
let some air through
open the windows will you
and the door.
He had had two halves of lager
Three days before.

____ He saw his dinner on TV _____

one day John cooked up his favourite
sausage chips and curried beans
and hurried into the living room
eager to consume the nourishment
he sat himself down in front of the telly
and his mouth fell open wide
there wasn't any food on his fork though
it was something on the screen
he was tellyfied
he'd never seen anything like it
well he had – that was the trouble
the sausage was the same sausage
the beans were the same beans
even the chips in the chips were the same
the plate was different – the cutlery was utterly
    different
but the dinner was exactly the same
the only occasion on which John had experienced
anything out of the ordinary before
was an occasion on which a letter came
through the door
that was actually meant for his nextdoor neighbour
but nothing like this
there was a knock at the door
it was John's new neighbour
she handed him a postcard
depicting detail for detail
the very bowl of jelly he had prepared for his afters
then John's dog walked in

a dog which incidentally he had buried the previous
   evening
that night John couldn't sleep
so he got up
and emptied a few marshmallows into a shallow dish
as a little treat for himself
there were seven of them – six white and one pink
and they looked so appetising
that John took a polaroid snapshot of them
as a kind of memento
he then plucked the pink marshmallow
sucked it
swallowed it
and turned to the photo to remind himself of his
   favourite
but there was no pink marshmallow in the photo

Steamed pudding

at our school you had to have everything
and you had to eat everything
and for some years
I would slip my steamed pudding in my pocket
disposing of it later in the playground bin
but one day I decided I was too old to behave like this
and I put my hand up and said please Miss
I can't eat this steamed pudding
and Miss said that I was mistaken
and I would have all lunch break
and after school if necessary
and possibly the rest of my life to prove it
she got back to her task of crossing out people's work
and left me with mine
it was slow – unpleasant
three quarters of an hour of held breath
and pretending to be anywhere but the present
but eventually there was no more steamed pudding to
    be seen
my bowl scraped as clean as someone who loved the
    stuff
neatly and quietly I put down my spoon
then she put down her pen
and smiled
not the smile she had when she was caning someone
but the smile of someone who has asked you
to demonstrate your love by doing the impossible
and unaccountably
it has been done

a smile as if she understood
how I hated steamed pud
I want to give you something for doing that she said
those mouthfuls weren't enough to feed a little mouse!
and I imagined an outrageous benevolence
possibly the confiscations of another boy
possibly a million points for my house
probably a joy beyond my imagining
she beckoned me close
and from out of her desk
she handed me a second helping

Bad news

when I used to write my daily news
I nearly always went over the page
and the boy sitting next to me never
for him three lines was a good endeavour
but one day he wrote three and a half pages
and he said to me SEE
you're not the only one who's clever
and he went and showed it to Miss
and Miss showed it to the class
look at all these words she said
they make no sense whatsoever

One day while we were getting out our rough books

one day while we were getting out our rough
    books
there was a bit of chattering
and Miss went all red and said stop stop stop
STOP STOP STOP
and we were very quiet
and Miss went more red and said
there is something the matter with the children
in class two purple
do you know what you are?
DO YOU KNOW WHAT YOU ARE?
and we were very very frightened
and we did not know what we were

The martian

there was a young creature from space
who entered a three-legged race
he was not very fast
in fact he came last
because he was a bag of oven-ready chips

The play

yesterday I went to see a play in my friend's car
it was by an experimental group
who do plays in people's cars

The snub

at school I used to play a lot of 'Subbuteo'
(a table football game)
and they used to call me Sub
and it was good to have a nickname
until they told me it stood for sub-standard

The scouting outing

there was Green Green
who fell in the latrine
and when Redman said to Green
let's go and dig a latrine
he didn't mean with shovels
he meant let's form a latrine appreciation society
and there was Joe
who brought his blow-football along
and there was Strong
who beat him every game
and there was one lad
who had never seen blow-football before
whose name I can't remember
and there was Tony Ward
whose folks couldn't afford a uniform
but he'd just got himself a paper-round
and anyway the campfire's warm
welcomed every colour creed and parental income
    bracket
and there was Skip Skip
with his artificial hip
and there was Joe
saying I don't know if I want to go
pulling out people's tent pegs
and there was Redman calling him a drip
and there was Dorking talking about sleeping
and keeping the peace by saying Joe
was nowhere near as big a drip as Green
(whose Dad was in the police)

there was a village shop to pillage
tuck under torchlight
and the never-ceasing porchlight of the tall frame tent
which meant our leader needn't crouch and crawl
and he could keep an eye out
through the little plastic windows in the wall
oh the joy of it all
on that boy scout jamboree
never having heard of the likes of CND
never doubting there'd be scouting for our children
with the jumbo campfire kettle
forever spouting tea
if they'd had a badge for being optimistic
I imagine they'd have given one to me

Skip

Dad's dark glasses

sometimes when my Dad was watching the telly
he would fall asleep
and my Mum would shake him and say
go to bed Bob will you if you're knackered
and he would wake up and try to look alert
but one day he said the glare from the telly was hurting
    his eyes
and he would need some dark glasses
and from that day on
you couldn't tell if he was asleep
or watching the telly

The wizard that was

his pointed hat is pointless
his magic wand's a stick
his dog could do better tricks with
if she hadn't run away
he can say every word the spell book says to say
and wave his arms about all day
but he's powerless
he couldn't cast a shepherd
in a school nativity play

The genie in the wireless

one day John turned on his radio
and heard a voice say hello I'm the genie in your
    wireless
if you're a genie why aren't you in a bottle?
John snapped at what he thought was another
    stupid advert
and slightly hurt the genie replied
you could say I've lost my bottle couldn't you John?
but only because you always tend to state the obvious
realising that the genie was probably real
John immediately demanded his three wishes
so you only want me for what you can get then?
enquired the lonely force
of course replied John indignantly
why else does anybody want anyone?
for what they can give?
suggested the genie
OK John replied so give me a great big car!
how beautifully humble remarked the machine's
    unseen ghost
how wholly imaginative
not like the last person who asked me for a piece of peanut
    brittle
and wanted to be the rainbow in the bubble
of a trouble-maker's spittle
that's right agreed the other slightly confused
nothing like it - I want a big car
and I want to be able to drive
all right but that's your lot said the voice in the radio

no it's not that's only one wish
two at the most John complained
and the genie explained about the cuts
in the magical services industry
and told him that there was a march if he
   was interested
the only March I'm interested in
is the one that comes after April
said John making a bit of a mistake

___ Mr McNaulty _____

one day Mr McNaulty left the launderette to get some
   fags
and these boys came in with laundry bags
and unloaded a number of small dogs
into one of the tumble driers
as they fumbled with the faulty coin mechanism
Mr McNaulty returned
OH NO YOU DON'T he cried
pushing them aside
and pulling out the dogs
these driers are for washing machine customers only

Skip

Train spotters

OK so some of us wear anoraks
and some of them have hoods with fur on
and some of us drink quite a bit of cocoa
but it doesn't mean we're loco

everybody's looking out for something
that may be round the bend
we just tend to do it with a duffle bag
but we're train spotters
we're not trend setters
and a platform ticket takes us
just as far as we want to go
– to the end of the platform show

is taking down another person's underwear
being any more alive
than taking down a one-two-five's little details?
OK so we may be wetter
but it is better than drying
the wet that you get from crying
over a love that is dying

is the happy shunter hunter
any more insane
than the lot who've not got jotters
who spot the spotty spotters
with disdain?
we're looking forward to our crusty rolls
we've got platform tickets

and platform souls
it's a passion
not a fashion show
it's smashen' though

___ Well bred dog _____

one evening John came home from work
went into the kitchen to make himself a nice cup of tea
and on the kitchen table in a plastic bag
he discovered a large sliced loaf with one of the crusts
   missing
actually it was a VERY large sliced loaf
about the size of a rabbit hutch
and John who lived very much alone
knew that he hadn't put it there and wondered who
   had
just then there was a rap a tat tat at the front door
it was John's new next-door neighbour
excuse me barging in she said
but you haven't seen my dog have you?
what does it look like enquired John concernedly
like a large sliced loaf replied the neighbour
with one of the crusts missing asked John
yes replied the neighbour she had a fight
John smiled
went out into the kitchen
and returned with the mysterious loaf
is this her by any chance he asked
and the neighbour said no
that must be somebody else's dog

Well executed poem

before the blast of the squad
his last request
was a bullet-proof vest
or a God

Electric chair poem

the volts
the jolts
the end

I am going

there is not a rumour
of humour
in the tumour
of our life
I am going
I am stifled
I am going
to survive
you would do anything for me
except go
it is me not you
who makes you feel alive
I am going
I'll be back about five

On the bus

for a while I was a bus conductor
and one day my Dad got on my bus
and sat on the long seat next to my cubby hole
he was proud to see me in a uniform and a job
and in a loud voice he said to everyone
do you remember the bus conductor's outfit you had
when you were a boy John?
and I said no Dad
but I remember how you used to enjoy beating me

Poetry

poetry don't have to be
living in a library
there's poetry that you can see
in the life of everybody,
a lick of paint's the kind of thing I mean
a lick of paint's a lovely piece of writing
the tongue of the paintbrush
giving something drab
a dab new sheen
a lick of paint's exciting.

there are folk who like to see
Latin in their poetry
and plenty of obscurity
me for instance
(only joking)
how I like to listen to the lingo
in bingo
legs eleven
clickety-click
a lick of paint
no – sorry that ain't one

poetry – language on a spree
I want to be
a leaf on the poetree
poetry is good for me
I think I'll have some for my tea

String

If you're depressed
and your life don't mean a thing
pop into a hardware shop
and cop hold of some string.

My old cap

Before I get sat in the café
I take my flat cap off my hair
and place it in the lap
of the uncharitable chair.
It makes a good little cushion
but unfortunately I leave it there.
I do not realise that this is where
I have left it, until a week's time
when I'm in the café once more
and my order is taken by a chap
who is jauntily wearing my cap.

Going to Virgin Records

On the underground
a man communicates in sign language
and I listen to the sound of his
anorak.

___ A spectacular tale ___

Once I had a whitehead on the bridge of my nose in the shape of a railway engine which made the wearing of my glasses uncomfortable, but being shortsighted, and because I was only doing close-up work at the time, I felt able to remove my old friends, placing them carefully into the home of their case, which in turn I positioned in the inside pocket of my shirt. During the next half an hour or so I ventured into no form of human bustle where someone might have interfered with the case and if an intruder had tried to sneak into the room taking advantage of my poor eyesight, my keen-eyed dog John would certainly have noticed and sounded the alarm. However when I did finally go out and I removed the case myself I discovered a pair of spectacles identical to the ones I had recently removed.

Only they were made entirely of plasticine!

A little story which I have given certain embellishment: the spot was not railway-engine shaped, the inside pocket of my shirt was of course a jacket pocket and, most significantly, I omitted to relate that on positioning the plasticine spectacles on my face, I experienced a terrible sense of my own mortality as it struck me that during my life I would only remove and replace my glasses a specific number of times. The thought filled me with sombreness to the extent that I began to weep, removing the glasses so that I could wipe my eyes, thus adding one more to whatever the final number would otherwise have been; the realisation of which cheered me to such an extent that I decided to take John for an additional walk around the house.

A walk around the house

you've been both a good dog and a bad dog
and I have got some good news and some bad
the good news is we're going for a walkies
but it won't be the longest walkies you have ever had

off we go then
here's the hall
no – we're not going out at all
there's the stairs
that's the way
let's be different
today

up we go then
not so fast
if you want this walk to last you
here's my bedroom
there's my pit
where's the walkies?
this is it

have a sit down
rest your paws
there's a bit of a mess
now – can you guess which bit of it is yours?

___ Smothering Sunday ___

To a wonderful mother
with wrinkly skin,
this card was concocted
by one of your kin.
I hope that you like it
it's specially for you,
I've sprinkled some glitter
on top of some glue.
I don't like the bought ones
I thought you should know,
they're too superficial
and two quid a throw
some of them.

The Easter Story
according to St Bernard

When they come to take his boss away
the apostle with the sword
smote the servant's ear off
and got told off by the Lord,
who replaced the lackey's lug'ole
saying not to be so rude,
but not before a naughty dog
had thought someone had given her
a little scrap of food.
And that undignifying Friday
when it seemed they'd sealed His doom
the dog that chewed the ear up
got to end up in the tomb,
and by the Sunday morning
she was dying to be fed
and she barked and she barked loud enough
to waken up the dead,
which she did.

On Hampstead Heath

I ask you what sort of tree
we are sat underneath
and you tell me that it is a big one.
You ask me how I came by the scar on my knee
and I tell you that I hurt myself once.
A passer-by, possibly Austrian
and possibly a Christian,
points to a fluorescent cycle clip in the grass
and wonders if I might have lost it.
I stand up and indicate that I am wearing shorts.

What we have been

We have been too eager
to learn each other's secrets
and now we're not so keen
we are like the wings of a moth
without the moth bit in between.

The photos of the divorce

The ones at the end
(after the flying saucers)
the ones of them coming apart,
they came out so much better
than the wedding pictures,
there was no confetti in the camera
for a start.

Making confetti

The North Yorkshire Moors Railway
in a coal-burning journey
fuelled by love and enthusiasm.
I collect my thick oblong of ticket
at the start
and an inspector's hole
in the shape of a heart
somewhere in the middle.

Train window pain

gazing through the glazing
glasses pressed on glass
sad eyes on the shining track
going back
to town

Off the rails

the ticket inspector said I'm a defector
but spoke like a native and broke into song
he sang about cricket while building a wicket
and Stephenson's 'Rocket' came rolling along

and out of the Rocket stepped old Davey Crockett
who waved to his mother and went in to bat
I'm cracking at cricket and I've got no ticket
he said showing off in his usual hat

the backwoodsman's Mum said I'm coming old chum
and she bowled an alarm clock from out of the blue
and the man at the sticks said I'll knock it for six
even though it's been set for a quarter to two

Crockett was out he was too busy talking
and as he was moodily walking away
the East German sector born ticket inspector
said if you've no ticket there's money to pay

the disgruntled Crockett dipped into his pocket
and in the confusion he ended his life
he threw down his hat and let go of his bat
and then slowly keeled over on top of his knife

the sky went all cloudy
his last word was howdy
his mother then said of the deed
oh what a business
my boy's lost his is-ness
the ticket inspector agreed

___ Camping for pleasure _____

After I'd gone on my first bit of camping with the
   scouts
I went to the public library and got a book out
called Camping For Pleasure
in which there was a bit about how to make
a trip to the toilet more comfortable
by taking a saw to the seat
of a worn-out wooden chair
and taking out a circle of the appropriate size.
After I had attempted to realise this contraption
my mother seriously contested my concept of worn-out
with reference to the kitchen chair of my choosing
that she was losing
and my father demonstrated that if nothing else
there was still plenty of wear left in the discarded seat
for beating purposes.

In Edinburgh

I'm in the Botanic Gardens gallery
a man pushes past me
to look at a beautiful picture
without saying pardon.
I want to point a sizzling finger
and make his arteries harden
to the stiffness of the depicted stone,
a feeling Festival artists are known
to have directed at the Press
which has been putting a picture
alongside the stinkingest review
to make the unwitting performer think
'oh look it's me'
and then be
particularly unpleasantly surprised
by the accompanying poison.

Christmas in the doghouse

It was Christmas day in the doghouse,
and no one had a bone,
and one dog who was desperate
was chewing up the phone-book,
when suddenly to their surprise
a canine Santa came
and luckily they had no logs
or he'd have been aflame.

Good news I bring the Santa said
('cos he knew how to speak)
from now on I'll be visiting the doghouse
once a week,
we'll break the human habit
they seem to hold so dear;
good will to fellow creatures,
but only once a year.
It's true we tend to urinate
around the Christmas tree,
but we're fit to lead
and not be led
in spreading Christmas glee.

They didn't want a sermon though
that's not why he was there
they all piled in like vermin
to his sack of Christmas fare,
and they eated all the bones up
and they treated Santa rough,
and as he left the doghouse
he said once a year's enough.

God plays I Spy

I spy with my little eye
something beginning
with sinning
that's not as nice as paradise
and I have to send my son down twice
to save it

The miracle and the people

the statue on the pilgrimage
is bleeding from the hands
and asking for a handkerchief
but no one understands
Latin any more

The Romans

they had planning restrictions
they had tenement flats with balconies
and café meeting places on the ground floor
they had central heating
central government
and fire brigades
they even had those little things
you put under indoor flower pots
to stop any spillage
when the plants have been watered

Watling Street

Just off the Old Kent Road
I dig them digging
in the archæological way
the Roman way to Chester,
these are shards of flagon
possibly flung from a passing wagon
I'm told.
The wine has dried,
the drinker's died
and here is the evidence,
the diamond spade delves
for everyday items
new diamonds themselves
to be placed on shelves
for the eyes of the people.
But I am informed that last night
that sight was shortened
as this site of diligent tillage
was unsettled and pillaged,
by pillocks with metal detectors.

Digging for it

Sometimes a poem is less of an invention
and more of a find
its birth a kind
of archaeology,
a job of unearthing and piecing together
and sometimes a piece won't fit
because it's part of something else,
and sometimes it is just a bit of old rubbish.

The pillars of the gods

In the dark ages
the remains of Roman extravagance
must have been a top-most mystery
to a population with such a lack
of building skills
and history teachers.
Who were these beings
with such a miraculous knack
of stacking stones?
Where did they go?
and more unnervingly,
when would they be back?

Sat on the Pillar of Hercules

I bought a book about Roman eroticism
with images and artefacts
the museums had banned,
just for research purposes you'll understand.

Forever Roman

Mile after Roman mile,
travelling from Newcastle to Carlisle,
in spite of seeing Hadrian's Wall
now fallen like the empire,
I imagined a Roman at that Empire's height
standing by the roadside
and seeing the way of the Romans
stretching to a distance
as far as this moment of mine.
A Roman with a future,
for whom the sun was equally high,
under an identical
blue sky.

Gaul

Once a Centurion soldier
said Venus how I want to hold yer
she replied I'm a god
and it's great on my tod
and his mate said Marcellus I told yer.

A centurion has a bit of fun

This centurion goes to a dance and for the first time in ages he lets others take the lead. Like a child with a rattle he is wild and unselfconscious, but the following morning he's rather stiff because him and all his hundred are killed like cattle on the battlefield.

The Roman ruins of Chester

On the last leg of the journey to Chester on 'The Sprinter' (which is like a sprinter with a bad leg) I see a hill fort and remember that the Romans were at Chester. During the evening's performance I am persistently heckled by a man with his legs over the empty seat in front of him. I point out to him that he is rather unlikeable; the audience seem to be in agreement and cheer menacingly like punters in a gladiatorial amphitheatre.

On leaving the hotel in the morning I have 35 minutes before my train is due to depart. I see a hackney taxi, hail it and tell the driver that I would like him to take me to the railway station, but first could he show me something of Roman Chester? He says there is the Amphitheatre and some Roman gardens and I am most agreeable. The Amphitheatre is rather unspectacular, a single layer of stones, little more than markers of what was once magnificent. But it IS Roman and touching the red stone makes me tingle. As we drive on, my impromptu guide points out the oldest pub in Chester and some Tudor carvings. I feel it would be rude to point out that I am not interested; I want to see Roman things. When he shows me the remnants of an abbey which he says was built before Roman times I do sit up rather and wonder if this can possibly be true. Who built it then? I enquire. The monks before the Romans came, I'm told. No – I think he must have got it wrong. Now these Roman Gardens, can I have a look at them?

He says he will have trouble parking but manages and as I enter the Gardens I pass two men painting the railings in boiler suits. I wonder what the Romans would have made of the scene.

They would probably have understood the paint, possibly some of the dialogue, but I think the boiler suits would have been very surprising. Inside the Gardens is an immense sense of peace and the remains of pillars which remain magnificent. I embrace them and for a momentous minute or so I hold History in my arms, then return to the taxi where I see I have clocked up one eighty. We drive to the station. I put three quid into the cobbled palm, enter the concourse and buy three copies of a postcard depicting the Roman Garden ruins. On the train I wonder what a Roman might think of the picture. Depends on the Roman of course, but say it was your average sort of bloke, a fairly intelligent painter and decorator say. He might think it was a painting of how the Roman Garden might appear after many centuries. He would obviously not see it as a photograph, the process being unknown. If he were to see a second postcard he would think the hand of a skilful copier was at work; on seeing a third he might become confused; on seeing forty thousand or so he might think you could use them as wallpaper.

The Coliseum

it was difficult to see
if you were sat at the back
it was more difficult
if you needed the kind of spectacles
which were yet to be invented
it was worse if you were the worse
    for wine
and even worse if you were cursed
with a row of very tall citizens
sat immediately in front
and even worse than that
if your medium-sized master
obtained a better view
by getting you to lie flat on the
    terrace
so that he could sit on your spine

The Roman showm'n

The Roman showm'n
informs the throng
that he would like it to be noted
that some of his better material is quoted
in the senate
in fact
one of them once asked him to script them a speech
and he said why don't you go and pen it
yourself Julius?
Although he admits to changing his mind later
when it was suggested
that alternatively he might prefer catering
for some ravenous lions.

He gets to his gigs in a chariot
just for a bit of display
and he starts with a song
that is reasonably strong
called Rome wasn't built in a volcano.

He's been all around the empire
and around it all again
from Sicilia to Jerusalem
and from Africa to Lutonium.

And he warns if they juggle with too many balls
they'll balls up the whole of the act,
then he stands there and juggles a solitary ball
saying this is how jugglers get sacked.

He's good on the spur of the moment
which is good when the heckling begins
he once told a group of inebriate Christians
how lucky they were that their sins
had already been died for.
This shut them up apparently.

Togas

when togas had gone out of fashion
Augustus tried bringing them back
and the trendier folk in the forum
would joke about people who wore 'em

St George's Day poem

I like old English inns
but not Ye Olde Worlde pretence
I like the Stonehenge circle
so much better than the fence.

I like an English apple
(the bit that's not the core)
I like the little chapel
up on Glastonbury Tor.

I don't like English butchery
I don't like English lamb
verging on the English vegetarian I am
I do like English haddock though
I think it should be said
but do they know they're English fish
especially when they're dead?
No. Oh nonny nonny no they don't.

I like the English countryside
and English country tea
and lots of English mustard
but not in Irish coffee.

I love my English country
and other countries too;
I won't order egg and chips
when I'm in Timbuctoo.
I do like egg and chips though
and sticks of Brighton rock

and when I fry myself an egg
I never use a wok,
do you?
No?
Good.

I like the English language
I like the word latrine,
it's somewhere to express yourself
where others might have been.

I like the English heritage
I like to hear archaic English folk songs
being sung in that distinctive nasal way
but not all day.

Maurice

A dog's complaint

They say a dog's a man's best friend
but not a dog's best friend's a man
it isn't that surprising
when you're only there to guard his van
an inch of wound-down window
it can drive you from your wits.

Sometimes a dog's called Rover
and sometimes he's called Rex
these names they are rubbish
and they're only for a certain sex;
humans like to know you
by the nature of your bits
and the rule is if they match,
you're not to touch each other's privates.

They're glad that we can understand
the substance of their talk,
a shame they think all we can say is
I think there's someone at the door
or master can I have a walk.
I like it in the open though,
rolling in the grass,
striking up acquaintances
and sniffing fellow creatures up the
trees where they have recently been past.

Haircut in Seville

He guesses that I'm English
and gets on with the job.
Without my spectacles
there is little to see in the mirror
and I reflect on the holiday so far:
the flight, the first day in the hired car
and the fright
from my friend's difficulty remembering
that the traffic in Spain
stays mainly on the right;
November sunbathing in Cadiz
and the business with the prawns
in the mountain town of Rhonda.
as I ponder
the barber
runs his razor round my neck,
I keep very still
and hope he doesn't harbour ill
about the plight of the Armada.

Sketches of Portugal

On the track back
from the ruins of Conimbriga
finding a fraction of exercise book
in familiar looking folds
I wonder about the old Romans again,
did they make parchment aeroplanes?

On the trains
the notices on the windows
say not to throw bottles out,
unlike their English counterparts
which prohibit mere leaning.

On the roads apparently
there are more disasters
than anywhere else in Europe,
on the streets
the boys are selling plasters.

A Barrow escape

My fortune was told me in Barrow
by someone called Old Madame Tarot,
she said danger is near
it was lucky to hear
'cos I ducked
and avoided an arrow,
but Old Madame Tarot wasn't quite so
   fortunate.

On the Isle of Man

I remember that here
it is bad to be gay,
and not within the law,
and I wonder if anyone's made jokes
about entering Douglas before.

Grange-over-Sands

When they had fallen asleep
in the great hotel,
the snow fell.
By the morning it had laid
and after their Cumbrian breakfast
they came out into the quiet flakes
and made
a snow dog.
Although it had no name or bone,
it had its own snowball
and a small snow owner
who seemed to be an infinitely patient man,
and what with the Woodland Walk
and the nearby Lakes
they found themselves agreeing
that it was a very good place
to bring a dog
into being.

Bury St Edmunds

Getting dark near closing
in the park of the abbey ruins
I enter the recreation ground.
It has been raining off and on,
all the children are gone
and I am tempted by the swings,
things I spent hours on
when my trousers went no lower than my knees.
A small go would do no harm I decide.
Settled into the ride
and aware that I am breaking the rules
I prepare for the possible appearance
of a hostile parkie.
Why shouldn't I be here?
I'm no more danger to the apparatus
than ten stone three
of heavyweight child might be!
How strict is the authorised age-range anyway?
If you're one second past fourteen
does that mean you're banned?
And if I had a mental understanding age of nine
maybe that would be fine, would it, eh?
Some way off a figure
rounds the corner with some keys,
before the shape gets any bigger
I spill from the still swinging swing
and scarper for the trees.

A childhood hobby

One of my earliest pieces of poetic inspiration
was giving the game of drenching pieces of
tissue paper in spit then flicking them with
our rulers the name of flobby gobby.

First sex

I was about six
the first time my mother told me
how it was bad to play with myself,
but I think she preferred it
to me playing with my sister.

___ Lucky Bags ___

A lot of my small boy's sweet money went on Lucky
    Bags:
a few pastel-coloured edible shapes
that smelt too much of scent,
one or two not too tasty toffees
and the occasional slightly bent sweet cigarette,
the incentive to buy a Lucky Bag was not the sweets.
The attraction was the small toy included in every unit.
Excitedly I would feel the bright paper packaging
seeking insight into the nature of the unknown novelty
getting disappointed if I thought it was a whistle of
    some sort
(which it often was)
but you were purchasing anticipation not realisation;
you handed over your threepence
in the hope of the thing you'd always wanted
even if you never knew what that was
you paid your money because one day
you may be lucky.
For some reason I can clearly recall
one bag in particular,
a Jamboree Bag it was actually
exactly the same concept
but with pictures of boy scouts on the outside:
it's a foggy frosty morning
I've done the feeling around
and it's definitely not a whistle
I rip a thin strip from the top of the bag,
in goes my hand

and slowly
out comes the mysterious gift.
It IS a whistle after all,
would be the easy answer,
but not necessarily true
because now I can no longer remember what I had
I no longer know
how lucky
I was.

___ Scottish country dancing _____

It was something in the delicacy of the footwork
which appealed to me
when I first saw them Scottish country dancing in
    assembly
and although I was a bit of a lad about the school
I knew that I too wanted to do this
so I roped a friend into going along to a lesson in the
    dinner hour
and when the teacher saw that it was us
she said that she sincerely hoped we had not come there
    to be stupid
I insisted that we were there to learn
and begrudgingly she let us join the class
and after a bit our feet began to get the idea
and I got such a thrill
from the thought of learning the skill's secret
I laughed out loud at the pleasure of it
and immediately she turned off the record and said
now get out the pair of you
I knew you'd only come here to be stupid

At home

At fourteen I was not seen
by the others in my form
to be normal.
In a classroom debate
Jonathan Hawkins once created great laughter
by addressing us all
as ladies, gentlemen and Hegley.
But things were different
down behind the goal at Luton Town FC of a
    Saturday afternoon,
my pre-match chatter
mattered as much as anybody's,
belittling schooltime sniggers were no more
this was something bigger than schooltime
and at the entrance of the sacred twelve
swarming after their warm-up footballs
and soon to be put to the test
I was there with the rest
I was one of the crowd
I was part of the roar
LUTON
LUTON
LUTON
urging them to score,
and louder than Jonathan Hawkins.

Plasticine glasses

When my pocket money went up
from threepence
to fourpence,
my Dad referred to the revised figure
as big boys' pocket money.
Before I saw through big boys' glasses
I was to be seen
in glasses made of plasticine;
more colourful and flexible
than my specs are now
and less likely to fly off
when my Dad gave me a jolly good shaking
like he did once
when I was dressed up as a bus conductor.

___ Sheds _____

Once more I'm on the tracks
on my way to Hastings
looking at the passing house-backs
and contemplating sheds:
ramshackle sheds
ship-shape sheds
sheds with burglar alarms
surprisingly tall sheds
I-thought-it-was-a-kennel-it's-so-small sheds,
they're all sheds;
except for the greenhouses.
I wonder if the Normans had sheds.
I don't suppose a pair of glasses
would have been much good to Harold
when it came to all the bloodshed.

Can I come down now Dad?

My first memory of the toilet
dates from the beginning of training in its use,
being sat over the bowl
and told that this was where a big boy went to
    the toilet
and not in his potty
and not in a nappy,
and I was unhappy
and I cried and said, 'Daddy I'm scared
I shall fall down the hole!'
But I must have beaten my fear of the toilet
    somehow
because I've never been worried
about falling down the hole since
except once when I was very depressed.

The stand up comedian sits down

the comedian climbs onto the stage
and truthfully points out
that the microphone smells of sick
so does your breath says somebody
get on with it says somebody else
please settle down
replies the comedian responding well
I'll start this routine if it kills me
there is an outbreak of cheering
at the mention of his death
get off says the one who said get on with it
and the comedian comes up with a line
so apt and incisive
that any further heckling is redundant
unfortunately he comes up with it
on the bus home